Will The
ELECTORAL COLLEGE
DESTROY
OUR
Democracy
?

by STAN ROGERS

ASA PUBLISHING CORPORATION
AN INNOVATIVE OUTSOURCE BOOK PUBLISHING HYBRID

BBB
100 YEARS
Advancing Trust Together℠

ASA Publishing Corporation
25 S. Monroe St, Monroe, Michigan 48161
An Accredited Publishing House with the BBB
www.asapublishingcorporation.com

Copyrights©2023, Stan Rogers, All Rights Reserved ®
Book Title: Will The Electoral College Destroy Our Democracy?
Date Published: 06.16.2023
Edition: 1 *Trade Paperback*
Book ID: ASAPCID2380881
ISBN: 978-1-960104-19-9
Library of Congress Cataloging-in-Publication Data

This book was published in the United States of America.
Great State of Michigan

Table of Contents

i

Part II

-The Change from the Old to the New-

Part III
-The Percentage Method-

Will The
ELECTORAL COLLEGE

DESTROY

OUR

Democracy

?

by STAN ROGERS

The Constitution and The Electoral College

PREFACE

We, as a country, elect our presidents and vice presidents every four years. Our first election was held in New York in April of 1789. History books explain that event to its fullest. This article explores the methods, the voting structure, the rules, and some of the unusual elections we have had in the last 100 years. Its theme is the Electoral College, the electoral vote, and the popular vote. The major question is why, out of 24 elections, have there been 18 of which the western half of the country's votes counted for nothing?

I try to answer questions like, "*Why* is an election over when one candidate receives 270 electoral votes? *Where* does the electoral vote come from? Do we really have two elections? *What* happens to the votes that are not counted *after* an election is won when one of the candidates receives 270 electoral votes?" This report explores *why* the 1948 presidential election was the, "Turning point for how we handle elections." Throughout the writing, if you do not ask, "Why are we still using this system?" Stop reading. You are not understanding the message.

There are three parts:

Part I: I try to explain the history of the Electoral College and the Constitution. I identify the players, the election systems used in the early days, and the two types of votes that are still used today. I compare the communications and transportation systems of the early times to today's systems.

Part II: I describe the 1948 presidential election in great detail. This was the beginning of 20th century technological developments, communication advances, and transportation improvements. In this Part, I explain and compare what was then to what is now. I use charts and graphical data from past elections and the 2016 presidential election.

Part III: I review the results of the 2016 presidential election and introduce a proposed plan of how the popular vote and the electoral vote could change the dynamics of our elections without dropping the use of the electoral vote. This plan will force election results to include a full country vote count before we have a president-elect. The popular vote count would mirror the electoral vote count that would reflect all the people's choices.

The bottom line is, to let all the people living under the rule of the laws of this country decide the leaders *of* this country. Let democracy sing.

PART I
The Electoral College

The subject material about to be presented is complex and very confusing to grasp and understand. The material is not new, and I can only conclude that anyone that has studied American history in high school is vaguely familiar with the subject. It came into use in 1789 and has been used until today. It is the *Electoral College*, and it is embedded in the writing of the Constitution. The timeline for this dissertation will cover the years from 1787 to 2022. The reason this topic is important to study is because of the events that came out of the 2016 and 2020 presidential elections.

Democracy is the power of the people, a way of governing which depends on the will of the people, therefore we have free elections by the people to elect our leaders. This is what our Founding Fathers wanted for us. Anyone that is qualified to vote must vote and for anyone that does vote, their expectations are that their vote will be counted and have meaning. I will try to prove that the 2016 election and excerpts from several other elections will show that, by continued use of the Electoral College, we will eventually destroy the very thing that democracy stands for. This is *not* what the Founding Fathers created or expected. It is *not* my desire to destroy or eliminate the Constitution but to suggest changes to the Electoral College that will make it relevant to today and the modern way of doing things.

I will open with what I am writing about with this question,

"If you follow presidential politics, which side of the Mississippi River would you want to live on during a presidential election?"

This is a strange question, but you might be surprised and upset by the answer.

I have asked many people what they knew about the Electoral College, and I received answers like, "I did not apply to that school when I graduated from high school," or, "We talked about it in high school, but I was more interested in girls." I think the answer that most people told me was, "I am not interested in politics, and I do not know what you are talking about." I was one of those people until the 2016 election. That's when I tried to read the Constitution to understand this thing called the Electoral College. The wording was such that I had to write out what I was reading in today's English to be able to understand it. When I got to Article II of the Constitution as shown below, my first thoughts were "*What the?!*" Reading and writing further I decided to offer my thoughts on this subject.

I have been voting for over 60 years and never noticed that when we vote for a president and vice president there are *effectively two elections*. There is the popular vote and the electoral vote. This is where we are free to vote for anyone that represents our beliefs. However, there is another vote, not a vote from one person but a group of people called electors, and their votes added together are called the electoral vote. Per the Constitution, each state is assigned a finite number of these voters that will help in the process of electing our leaders. This will become clear and disturbing later. Let's get started and see where it takes us.

The Constitution of the United States

Article I, Section 4, Paragraph 1 of the Constitution of the United States

"The Times, Place and Manner of holding Elections for Senators and Representatives shall be prescribed in each State by the Legislature thereof; but the Congress may at any time by Law make or alter such Regulations, except as to the Places of chusing Senators." This is where the Constitution said that the states will hold these elections, but Congress can step in and make changes.

Article II, Section 1, Paragraph 1 of the Constitution of the United States

"The Executive Power shall be vested in a President of the United States of America. He shall hold his Office during the Term of four Years, and together with the Vice President, chosen for the same Term, be elected, as follows"

—Note: Amendment 22 has extended and limited his term to two terms as president with eight years maximum time in office. Some of their duties will be explained later.

Article II, Section 1, Paragraph 2. of the Constitution of the United States

"Each state shall appoint, in such Manner as the Legislature thereof may direct, a Number of Electors, equal to the whole Number of Senators and Representatives to which the state may be entitled in the Congress: but no Senator or Representative, or Person holding an office of Trust or Profit under the United States, shall be appointed an Elector."

—Here the Constitution sets the number of electors to be the same as the number of congressmen as for each state. It also proclaims that no Congressman or public servant can ever be an elector.

The electoral process is very involved and takes on several layers of action. When a territory wants to become a state, they must first ratify the Constitution before they are able to hold an election and vote for a president. See Page 45 for a list of when all the states ratified the Constitution. The original 13 colonies ratified the Constitution on June 21, 1788. Our first election was held on April 30, 1789, in New York City. George Washington and John Adams, among others, ran for president. Because Washington received the most popular votes he became president, Adams came in second therefore he became vice president. That is how elections were held then.

History played a major role in how the structure of an election evolved. It started with the formation of the Congress. In 1783 we fought and won the Revolutionary War to get away from English rule, but ironically, we adopted their model of government. Our congress is patterned after the English Parliament. Our House of Representatives is their House of Commons. Our Senate is their House of Lords and our President is the equivalent of their King. Using this backdrop and the building of the Constitution we will be able to see the rationale of the Electoral College and why we have it.

There are three "Branches" that make up the government. The Executive Branch is made up of the president, vice president, and the Cabinet. The Legislative Branch is made up of the House of Representatives and the Senate. The Judicial Branch is made up of the Supreme Court and lower courts.

The Executive Branch

President and Vice President This branch of the United States Government involves the Office of the President and his Cabinet. The president has the final say over the laws passed by the other Legislative branch. The vice president is there if the president can no longer serve due to death or removal.

The Legislative Branch

House of Representatives Each state has a finite number of representatives. The number of representatives a state has is equal to the number of voting districts it has. The process that determines the number of representatives a state has will be discussed when we talk about voting districts.

Senate Each state has two senators. In many states they are from each party, however, there are some states that the senators are from the same party. At this point in history, there are only two national political parties that are in each state.

Voting Districts A voting district is an area within each state defined by boundaries setup by the state. The processes and rules used to determine this array of areas in each state that defines the boundaries of a voting district are beyond this report. We will see that when there is population growth or shift in the population within that state the number of voting districts can change as it did in our country from 1787 to today. The importance of the voting district will become apparent as we progress.

National Census The word *census* is defined as an official count or survey of the population shift within a state. It is mandated by the Constitution that every ten years all the states shall conduct a census and the results be used to define the political geographical areas for each state known as voting districts. This count will define the areas where the people are living in the state and the population growth to the state. This information is then used to determine the number of voting districts needed for that state. If the number of voting districts grows then the House of Representatives will grow accordingly. In the early years, the number of people that defined a voting district was about 30,000 people. In the 1910 census that number rose to 212,000 inhabitants, and the current number, per my Smartphone Encyclopedia, is about 710,000 for the last census. All this means is that now *one* *representative* is responsible and speaks for over seven hundred thousand people in the state he lives in.

California is a good example of what happens from population growth. When the Western migration of people in the late 1800s through the early 1900s hit California, it changed their political makeup by increasing the number of representatives that went to Congress. In 1865 California had five voting districts. Today there are 55 voting districts and because of that California now has 55 representatives in Congress and *55 electors assigned to the state.*

As a side note, *political gerrymandering* runs rampant whenever a census is taken. This is when political parties try to change the district's boundaries to incorporate more supporters.

The geographical size of a state does not affect the number of voting districts a state has. It is determined by where the population clusters are in the states. There will be more voting districts around large cities than there are for rural parts of the state. All 50 states that make up the United States follow the same model to determine voting districts. An example would be to compare the state of New Jersey to the state of Montana. Today New Jersey has 14 voting districts while Montana has only three. Unless there is a massive population movement to Montana there will always be only three voting districts there. The number of districts does not change, but the number of people living in a district can. By knowing how many voting districts a state has we will always know how many representatives it has and how many electors it has.

Today there are 438 voting members in the House of Representatives in Congress for the *whole country.* Knowing that there are 50 states and that each state has two senators per state we know that the Senate has 100 voting members. Having 438 House of Representatives and 100 Senators we know that there are 538 voting members in the United State

Congress today. That same number is how many *electoral votes* the country has. Remember that number 538, 269 *is one half* of 538. The number **270** will be the most important number that affects today's elections.

The Electors Because Article II, Section 1, Paragraph 2 of the Constitution identifies how many electors there are to be for each state, the reason *why* they are there must be explored. It identifies their number to be the same as the number of congressmen in Congress. We know that when a state's population increases their number of representatives may grow, therefore so will the number of electors for that state. Electors are chosen, not elected. The political parties that represent a candidate for president can pick and choose the electors that the state is allowed to have. This number is true for any political party in any state that has a candidate for president. At that time the state will make sure that each elector that is picked can meet all the states requirements set down for electors. Electors come from all walks of life. The only time we use electors is when we hold our presidential elections every four years.

We cannot lose sight that from 1492 to 1789 most of the people that were settling in this country had never experienced an election. There was a need for people that knew the election process and what was needed to run a fair election. I think that the architects of the Electoral College created the electors because they knew that they would be needed to conduct an election and become the "teachers" for this process. The Electoral College and the electors have become an important part of the 57 presidential elections held for over the last 230 years.

In the early years, the electors were the people that knew what an election was and how to organize one. This task was anything but simple. Elections were held in large metropolises, small cities, villages, and rural townships, similar to what an election is today. Electors handled all the details then. Today, state's election boards handle this now, but on a much larger scale. Details like posting of times and places where elections would be held, procuring materials, and getting people to help run the elections became a big part of the process. The dates for national elections were chosen by the first Congress. It was decided that the first Tuesday after the first Monday in November would be best because that was a time when people were done preparing for winter. They would be gathering together after the fall harvest and celebrating. This became the best time to hold elections because more people could be involved.

After a state election was over, all the electors for all the candidates would gather the votes from all the voting places around the state and meet at a predetermined location within the state and count the votes. This process took time. I do not have any history of what goes on in these sessions, but I am sure that the counting process was organized so that there was no room for cheating. Once the counting of the votes was completed and a president-elect chosen, only those electors who were committed to the winning candidate will continue the process laid out by the Electoral College.

After all of the state's popular vote was counted, those electors that were picked by the winning candidate from each state received the state's electoral votes to be submitted to Congress for a state-by-state accounting. The votes submitted are the electoral votes, not the popular votes that the people cast when *they* voted for the winning candidate who won the state election. Each elector was assigned one vote then he/she gives a *sworn oath* to the candidate that chose them to be an elector and to the election officials of the state that qualified them, that they will submit their one vote for that candidate only. Sometimes they *do not do this*. They may give their *one electoral vote* to other candidates or they may not give it to anyone. There is a name given to those electors that do not report their one vote to Congress. They are called *faithless electors.* Their action is not illegal or punishable, only unethical. In the 2016 election there were five to seven *faithless electors* that betrayed their sworn oath. We will visit that election later.

In explaining the role of an elector, I have used words like electoral vote and processes that explain what an elector does before and after an election is held. Later, I will explain the main reason why the Electoral College should be changed or not used today. I will come back to the 2016 election process later.

POPULAR VOTE / ELECTORAL VOTE

TWO ELECTIONS IN ONE

The reason for this dissertation is because of the outcome of the 2016 election. I was irate when I heard that the losing candidate of this election received over two million *more* popular votes than the winning candidate did and still lost the election. Also, the fact that the winning candidate won the election before the voting was completed in many states west of the Mississippi River added to making me more upset. We will see later that *even when someone has voted, their vote may not have any value.* If we look into the Constitution and study the section on the Electoral College, we can find answers as to why this happens.

But why do we allow it to happen *today*? The deeper I looked for answers the more I needed to find out *why*. Why did the brilliant men of the times give us this document that has been a beacon for all of us and the rest of the world to follow, *ever* come up with a system like this.

Popular Vote

Electoral Vote

Winner-Take-All Elections

Popular Vote Today the popular vote, the "people's vote," belongs to anyone that is a citizen of the United States. They must be a resident of the state they are registered to vote in, and they must be 18 years old. These people *can* vote for the leaders that govern us. However, I found in 1787 the requirements were different. You had to be a citizen, 21 years old, and you must be a landowner. Voting was limited to men only. Women and slaves were not allowed to vote at all. After the Civil War and the slaves were freed, those that could read a little *were* allowed to vote. Depending on how little they could read there was always someone that "would *help*" them to vote. Women were not given the right to vote until after the *19th Amendment was ratified on August 18th 1920.*

On Election Day All 50 states, plus Washington DC, hold elections and the people from those states vote for the candidate that is best aligned with how they want their leadership to represent them. . The total popular vote count for each state election, for each candidate, are added together and recorded as the total popular vote for the country. From this number the candidate that received the most popular votes wins the election. "The people have spoken." *No! This is not true!!!*

Electoral Vote We have seen the words elector, Electoral College, and now the electoral vote. Earlier I explained that one of the duties of the electors is to present his/her vote to congress after an election. The electoral vote is a number that each state has and that is the number of electors that are derived from the number assigned by the Constitution in Article II, Section 1, Paragraph 2. Paraphrasing from that paragraph, *Each state will appoint a Number of Electors that is equal to the number of congressmen for that state.* Paragraph 3 goes on to say, *"those electors shall meet in their respective state and VOTE."* The number of votes each state has will be discussed later. The electoral vote and how it is used in our presidential elections is *a reason* the Electoral College is out of date.

Referring to Paragraph 2 of Article II of the Constitution, we know that each state shall have electors equal to the number of congressmen that state has. We know that the number of congressmen each state has is equal to the number of voting districts assigned to each state. The number of voting districts for the whole country is 538. If the number of electors is equal to the total number of congressmen, then the number of electoral votes must be 538. That number is current for the United States today. In 1789, when Washington won his election there were only 69 total electoral votes for the country. He received them all.

In the 2016 election the total electoral vote count was 538. The winning candidate only needed 270 votes, one more than half of the 538 votes available to become the president-elect. This means that the 538 electoral votes assigned to the electors, have more value than the popular vote given to the people of this country. Later we will see that the key to winning a modern presidential election is the electoral vote.

At this point, because the popular vote and the electoral vote are intertwined in one election we must explore *why*. Turn to Page 46 and review the part of the page that shows the electoral vote count for all the states, both east and west of the Mississippi River. We have gone over how the numbers came about and that each state's number of voting districts are equal to the number of electors and electoral votes each state has.

I will use Michigan's election as an example to explain the value of the electoral vote and the popular vote. On Election Day for the 2016 election over four million Michigan voters from both parties voted. Trump received 11,612 more popular votes than Clinton. That difference went to Trump and he won the

Michigan election. Because he won this state's election, he *received all* 16 electoral votes Michigan had to offer. Turn to Page 48 and find the results for the State of Michigan shown there. Note that the 16 EVC (electoral vote count) from Michigan are assigned to Trump. Looking across to Page 49 and note Clinton's EVC column there is nothing. This is because the candidate that wins the popular vote in a state election will receive *all* the electoral votes for that state. This is called a *"winner-take-all"* election. At the bottom of the EVC column is the total electoral vote count for the time zone. The explanation of what happened for Michigan's election is the same for all the other state elections, except for Nebraska and Maine. These elections will be discussed later.

The first presidential election was to elect George Washington, in 1789. That election was the same, but different from today's elections. The public voted for two or more men and the one that received the most popular votes would become the president. The candidate with the second highest popular vote count became the vice president. George Washington became our first president and John Adams became the first vice president. There were 13 colonies at the time, only six recorded any popular vote for the running candidates. The total number of popular votes cast in that election was 30,041. Washington received 24,750 and John Adams got 5291. All 13 colonies/states had already been assigned their electoral votes and the total for the 13 colonies was 69. Washington received all 69 electoral votes, even those from colonies that did not turn in any *popular votes*. The question that can be asked is, "Did Washington get his win from the 24,750 popular votes *or* was it from the 69 electoral votes he received?"

It is time to talk about *how* we conduct elections today and *why* we do it this way. We arrive at a polling place to vote for the person whom we want to be our national leader for the next four years. Where we go to vote is the same place we are registered to vote. By doing this it can be proven, on the spot, that we met all the requirements to vote. We are handed a paper ballot that has all the candidates' names that are running for the Office of President. The names on the ballot have been divided into political parties so that we can vote for our choice for president as a party member or as an independent voter for the candidate we like best. We make our choices with the confidence that *we* are helping to elect that person.

The votes cast for state elections are popular votes and the results for *both* candidates are being collected and recorded. However, as I just explained using Michigan as an example, the popular votes decide the *state elections* for both candidates. Votes cast from both parties cancel out each other's votes and those votes that do not get canceled become the deciding factor as to who wins the state's election and the total electoral vote count for that state. Think about what is happening here. The 11,612 popular votes for the Michigan election that Trump won, which did not get canceled, won that state's elections and *all* the electoral votes it had to offer. This difference factor is the same for all the states. Again, one can ask, are the candidates collecting popular votes for the win *or* is the real prize the state's electoral votes? We will get a better picture when we analyze *all of* the 2016 state election results. Found on Pages 48 – 53.

The National Time Zones

The national time zones were established in 1883, 94 years after the Electoral College came into being. There is a map on Page 47. Note the clocks that span from the East Coast across to the West Coast. Starting from the east progressing toward the west the zones are marked, EASTERN, CENTRAL, MOUNTAIN and PACIFIC. Alaska and Hawaii have their own time zones, respectively. Note the clocks: Starting with the Eastern clock it is 4 pm, the Central time is 3 pm, Mountain time is 2 pm, and it is 1 pm for the Pacific time. In Alaska it is noon, and it is 11 am in Hawaii. These one-hour differences will have a great effect on our elections.

How does this affect elections? When the voting polls open at 8 am EST on the Atlantic Coast it will be 5 am PST on the Pacific Coast. The voting polls in the PST zones will not open until three hours later. In Hawaii, polls open *five hours* after polls on the East Coast open. As stated, democracy lives when *all the people* have an opportunity to choose the government that they want to lead them. It would not be until the mid-1900s that the time zone factor would have an effect on the voting pattern for this country, but it *would* have an effect.

Back at our election polls in the EST, it is 8 am. We are ready to vote for the person who we want as our national leader for the next four years. The polls in the rest of the country have not yet opened. An hour later in a small town located somewhere in eastern Illinois it is 8 am CST and the voting process will start there. All the polls in the CST will now allow voting. This same process will begin at 8 am in the MST states and they will start their voting process. At 11 am EST, it will be 8 am in the PST. They too, will start voting. In the earlier elections, until 1883, there were no time zones, just the sun. When the sun came up in the state you lived in, that was the time all the voting took place, voting stopped when the sun set. It should be noted here that this process was the clock for most people at that time. Today there are lines on a map that tell us where the time zones are.

The 8 pm closing of the polls across the time zones will follow the sun as it starts to set. When the EST polls closed the CST will still have one more hour of voting, the MST has two hours voting time, the PST has three hours left, and all the way out in Hawaii they will have six hours left *for voting* . Referring back to the EST when their polls closed at 8 pm, many of the states in that time zone will have results and trends that will exhibit the outcomes of their elections. In earlier times this information was not available and did not mean much to the voters because the lines of communication were not there. Communication and transportation will be the topic of discussion later.

In earlier times, after *all the* polls closed across the country, the counting of votes and declaration of winners could take several days before the voting public knew the results of the elections. This all changed after the 1948 election. Reviewing the data from the 1948 election and the 2016 election will bring this concern with the time zones more into view as to how they affect an election. The 2016 election will show why we *should* change the election processes used today.

The 2016 Election

Turn to Pages 48-53 and follow how each time zone tracked the state-by-state results. After the polls closed at 8 pm in the EST, the candidates for the 2016 election, Trump and Clinton, had already been declared winners in the 22 states that are located in the EST. Trump won 10 states. He received 147 electoral votes and 31,619,955 popular votes. Clinton won the other 12 states and gathered 105 electoral votes. She won 33,781,143 popular votes. At this point in the election, Trump had 147 electoral votes and Clinton had 105. Clinton had 2,162,188 more popular votes than Trump, however Trump had 42 more electoral votes than Clinton.

The other two time zones were still voting at 8 pm when the polls closed in all the states in the CST and they started reporting their results. The total number of states Clinton won in the CST was two, and from those results she received only 30 electoral votes and 15,817,796 popular votes, bringing her total electoral votes count to 135 and her popular vote total to 49,598,939. Trump received a landslide of electoral vote counts by winning 14 of the 16 state elections in the CST. His popular vote count of 19,600,410 votes from winning the 14 state elections brought his collective popular vote count for both time zones to 51,220,365. The 128 electoral votes that he won in this time zone added to the 147 electoral votes won in the EST gave him 275 electoral votes. This is where I said earlier that the number 270 was important. The 275 electoral votes that Trump just earned because of two time zones totals made him the *president-elect for the 2016 Presidential Election.*

Here is where the *story* is the story. What this means is that because Trump received *275 electoral votes at this time halfway through the election*, Clinton cannot get more than 263 because, 538 - 275 = 263. Remember when I said that half of the 538 total electoral vote count would be important? 270 is one more than half of 538, therefore the 275 electoral votes Trump received, by the rules of the Electoral College, made him the 2016 president-elect.

Article II, Section 1, Paragraph 3: The person having the greatest Number of votes shall be the President, if such Number be a Majority of the whole Number of the Electors appointed 270 is one more than half of the majority of the total of 538 electoral votes. This is another case where the popular vote, by itself, is not used to elect *anyone.*

Where I see the biggest "negative" in the Electoral College system is that it is hypocritical to the meaning of democracy. We have a president-elect before the election is over. Any additional voting *cannot change* the outcome of this election. Even though the 2016 election was won, it was *not* over. The voting cannot be stopped and those voters will still be voting until the polls close in the MST and PST zones. Those votes are part of this election and their votes should have been counted to decide the winner.

This is where we see that the electoral vote count is the deciding factor to elect our presidents. The popular vote must still go on until all the states, in the MST and the PST have their votes counted and recorded. But the popular vote and the electoral votes won by either candidate from these state elections will have *no* effect on this election *because it has already been decided.*

The voting results in the MST gave Trump *27 more electoral votes* making his total count at that point 302. His popular vote count total for this time zone was 4,467,449 and therefore increased his popular vote total to 55,687,814 for the three time zones. Clinton's share of the popular vote of 3,752,215 for this time zone raised her total for the three time zones counted to 53,350,554. The 14 electoral votes for the MST brings her total electoral vote count to 149. The difference in the total popular vote of 2,337,260 is in Trump's favor and the fact that he now has 302 electoral votes makes it a certain win for him. As a sidenote, the total votes cast for both democrats and republicans for the MST was equal to 8,219,664. Because the election is over, these votes have *no value* to either candidate. It should be proof enough that this is *not what the founding fathers wanted.* But wait, there is *more.*

Finally, the polls close in the PST and here is where the wheels come off for me. By this time the computers across the country have it that Trump already won the presidency two hours earlier. The polls did close and the final results stunned many people.

Of the six states in the PST Clinton won five of them and she received 84 more electoral votes, bringing her total electoral vote count to 233 for the election. Trump won one state in that time zone, Alaska, and received three additional electoral votes that brought his total electoral vote count for the election to 305. Trump's total popular vote count for the PST was 7,294,252, making his total popular count for the election *62,982,066.* Clinton's total popular vote for this time zone was 12,421,317, bringing her total popular vote count for the election to *65,771,871.* Clinton won *2,789,805* more popular votes for the 2016 election than Trump did. *But* none of this made any difference because the election was over by 8 pm in the CST and Trump was the winner.

The Electoral College must be changed to fall in line with today's standards and not those of the late 18th and 19th centuries. I chose to highlight the 2016 election for several reasons. First and foremost, the numbers just shown are not the democracy that the dictionaries define, *as a system of government by the whole population or all the eligible members of a state.*

First, is this the democracy that we want the world to know exists here in the United States? Second, how can we, as a population, cast 128 million popular votes for the candidates of our choice, and then have 538 electors pick our president when *the votes* of the people elect someone else. Ironically, in the 2016 election it did not take 538 electoral votes to override the over 128,000,000 *people's votes*. It took only 275 electors' *assigned* votes to win this election. This is not the democracy the Founding Fathers wanted for us.

PART II

The Change from the Old to the New

1948 Presidential Election

Communications and transportation across the country were improving at this time. World War II had ended, thousands of soldiers were home or coming home. The number of people that owned a television set was growing all around the country. The need for better roads was becoming a necessity and the use of computers was on the rise. It can be argued that things started to change in the 1948 election. It has been said that the 1948 election was lost and then won because of television and its use in a national presidential election. This election had some other twists that are also relevant to this subject of why the Electoral College should be changed.

The 1948 election was the first election after the second World War. The Twenty-Second Amendment was passed by congress in 1947 limiting the terms of all presidents to only two terms, or eight years in the office as president. This amendment was ratified by all the states on February 27, 1951.

Vice President Truman became president on April 12, 1945 because President Roosevelt had passed away. Truman became a candidate for president in the 1948 election. The 1948 election was the first time television was used for broadcasting national campaigning events, showing election proceedings and projecting results during Election Day. Computers were being used for gathering data and early predictions of results that were later broadcast on TV on Election Day.

There was another element to this election that could have affected its outcome and introduced a process very seldom used in today's elections. In this election there were three candidates running for president: Truman, who was vice president at that time, Thomas Dewey, who was the governor of New York, and there was a third candidate, named Strom Thurmond, who was a third-party candidate for the States' Rights Democratic Party. The votes that Thurmond *could win* would reduce the number of electoral votes available to the other candidates, who needed to get to 267 electoral votes, which was one more than half of the 531 total electoral votes *needed to win* the election that year.

On election night the counting of ballots for the country was going on. It was 9 pm in the EST states, and the polls had just closed in the CST states. There was an hour of voting left in the MST states and two hours of voting in the PST zone. Dewey was already leading with around 170 electoral votes. He needed only another 96 electoral votes to win the presidency. Television reports also had Thurmond's electoral vote count at 39. Truman was in the race but computers were predicting that he did not have much of a chance to win. Truman saw this, conceded the election, and went to bed around 11:00 pm EST knowing that he was losing the election. It should be noted that at this time, this was the first presidential election that this much information was available to the voting public on the *day* of the election. Everyone that was following the television reports knew that the morning headlines for the major papers across the country were going to read, "Dewey Wins."

By 4 am the *next morning* all votes were in for the *whole country*. Truman had received 24,179,347 votes, 49.6 % of the total popular vote, and with that he received 303 electoral votes. Most of his support came from the western states. Dewey received 21,991,292 popular votes, 45% of the total count and only 189 electoral votes. Thurmond's popular vote count ended at 1,175,930 votes, only 2.4% of the total votes cast and he never got more than 39 electoral votes total. There were 47,346,569 popular votes cast in this election. Everyone that voted for Truman had their vote counted, which helped to elect him president. The total electoral vote count for that year was 531. This was one of the eight elections, out of 230 years of elections, in which a president was elected because all the votes, popular and electoral, across the country, were counted and needed in order to elect a president. For the 1948 election, ALL the states' votes counted for the win.

"What if" Thurmond's electoral vote count had reached 80? All he had to do was win Texas' 38 electoral votes then Truman's count would have been reduced to a number less than 266. That year the Electoral College was at a total count of 531 because Alaska and Hawaii had not yet become states. *If* the electoral vote was split between three candidates, conditions would have existed that no one would have had enough electoral votes to become president. The presidential election would then have to be settled by the House of Representatives. This is called a *contingent election; it is only used when there is not a majority win of the electoral votes.* If that had happened then the House of Representatives, per the requirements of the Electoral College, would be the deciding vote for electing a new president. The Senate would then vote for the vice president. That year the Congress was controlled by the democrats and if it had become a contingent election, Truman still would have been elected because of that reason. Another problem with a contingent election and maybe a worst-case scenario, would be that the Senate *could* elect someone from the other party to be vice president. This has never been tried before, but I do not think it would ever work. There have been elections before that had more than two candidates, but the candidates that became the president-elect in those elections have had enough *electoral votes* to win.

The 1948 election had another twist to it. This was the *first election* where TV and computers played a major role on Election Day. Presidential elections, starting from the 1790 election until the 1944 election, were basically the same. There would be an election, and after *all the votes were in and the polls closed*, the vote counting process would begin. Because of the communications of the day, no one would have known who won the election until that process was completed. This sometimes could take as many as two weeks before any information got out to the voting public.

In every presidential election held since 1948, the computer has been used to collect real-time data and television would broadcast it immediately. This data can be used throughout Election Day to show how each candidate is doing, and because of television the final results can be reported at the end of the election on the day of the election for the whole world to see. I do not think the Founding Fathers had had any idea it would be this way over 230 years ago.

Technological developments after 1948, offer *more reasons why* some things must change, or we will be writing about the downfall of our democracy and what could have prevented it. Since the 1948 presidential election, television does in minutes what took days in earlier elections to bring ongoing information to the people. Numerical information and analytical results are handled by computers and because of television, this information can be broadcast immediately to the world. There is no comparison to the timelines for today as to what they were before 1948. Just the handling of data can best be summarized by realizing that we can now send information and data electronically to where it is needed immediately, instead of physically having to transport it to a location where electors and state election workers can work on it and arrive at the same results.

But we still do it today!!! The topics that we just covered explained the *physical reasons* that the Electoral College is obsolete and should be changed.

Everything presented so far has had to do with how the rules for the Electoral College are in place and the reason why we have electoral votes, winner-take-all elections, and only 538 electors that each have one vote assigned to them that count to elect our president. The reality of the whole thing is that it takes only one vote more than half of 538, (270), to elect our presidents. This is what happened in the 2016 election, and sixteen other elections in the last 100 years, and it will happen again. See Page 53 for a graph showing those results. The conditions the Founding Fathers had to work with in 1787 were *not* what we have today. Let's talk about conditions that *did not* exist in 1787, *but do now.*

Logistics

Transportation

Communications

Logistics In 1787 the 13 original colonies stretched from Maine to Georgia. The distance between these two colonies is about 1200 miles. The population at this time was over 400,000. There were hundreds of villages and cities that needed to hold elections and report the results. As mentioned earlier, this is where the electors were needed to set up our elections and report the results. Today the population of America is over 350 million people. There are 50 states where people make their homes, from the Atlantic to the Pacific Oceans, from the Canadian border to the Mexican border. America now is made up of almost 4,000,000 square miles. The systems needed and used to hold an election today and the dynamics involved to do so have changed in the last 230 years.

Transportation In 1787 the ability to move around was limited to walking, horseback, or horse drawn carriages. Good roads were nonexistent. Before 1789 the center of government was located in Philadelphia. After George Washington became president, Congress changed the location to Washington DC.

This made life for those people that handled the day-to-day requirements of governing very difficult because traveling was very difficult. The railroads were nonexistent until 1830. When they started being used for public transportation their top speed was limited to six to eight miles per hour. During this time the trips from Maine to DC or from Georgia to DC could not be done in less than seven days. Using today's modes of transportation, those same trips using the available mobile equipment can be completed sometimes in less than two hours. Today's automobiles can travel over 700 miles on good roads in eight hours. Trains can travel 2000 miles in three days and airplanes can travel that same distance today in less than three hours. The availability of all this equipment is there for anyone to use.

Communications In 1787 communication was limited to a few printing presses, handwritten letters, and word of mouth in order to inform the public of where and when an election would be held. Reporting the results of an election to the voters would be a repeat of the same. It wasn't until the 1860s that the printing presses and the Pony Express made those processes a little easier and faster. It is assumed all of the states held their elections at that time, on the same day. Due to the limited communications of the day this meant that all the results would not be known until days after their elections.

With today's communication a *projected* winner of any election can be broadcast to the *whole world* the same day of the election *before* all the election polls close across the country. For today's elections, the *when* and *where* factor is handled by newspapers and television reports. Gathering and reporting results are handled by computers and television on the same day as the elections. Today, we can vote in Miami, Florida, at 1 pm and with our cell phones call our brother in Portland, Oregon, and then tell him who we voted for while he is on his way to vote at 9 am the same day. The results for both actions will be reported that evening.

These quick glimpses of history over the past 234 years allowed us to see how the logistics, transportation, and communications of today have changed and how elections are intertwined together in order to allow the voting public to elect our leaders. Again, the question must be asked, *why* are we still using a voting system like the Electoral College to hold our elections today?

Turn to Page 54 and review the data on that page. Examine the columns as explained on Page 55. Note the column labeled "TIME ZONE," and count the number of elections that were won in the EST and CST zones. Until 1948 the time zones did not have the effect they do today because election results were not reported until days after the elections were over. In the "Winner EV" column, the electoral vote count for the winning candidate, if the number is over 300, he would have received at least 270 of them before the 8 pm closing of the CST voting stations.

Note the years 1932 through 1944. Follow over to the time zone column and see that those elections were *all* won in the EST. As I just wrote, the time zones were developed in 1883. The time of day did not affect the voting process until the mid-1900s because of lack of communication. Jumping to the 1948 election the problems of the past were getting solved. People were able to move around better, information was available and got to the people faster and things like election results were available to all much faster.

Time Zone Factor and Winner-Take-All

We have already discussed these factors but let's look and see how they support each other. The time zone factor cannot be changed. The electoral votes, assigned to each state, are the *prize*, and this *prize* reflects other issues of our elections. We have already seen that when a candidate wins the popular vote for a state, he will be the *winner-take-all recipient* of *all* the electoral votes that state has to offer. States like Pennsylvania and Michigan, having 20 and 16 electoral votes each, are states that both parties want to win. There are 26 states, plus Washington DC, that are east of the Mississippi River, shown on Page 34, that will produce as many as 308 electoral votes, 38 *more* votes than are needed to bring a candidate the 270 vote count needed to become the president-elect for that election. There are 24 states west of the Mississippi River that will produce 230 electoral votes. The information on Page 28 shows that in the last 100 years the presidency was decided in 19 out of 27 elections solely by states in the eastern and central time zones.

The Eastern Vote Count If one candidate were to win 27 states east of the Mississippi River, he/she would win 243 electoral votes and would need only 27 more electoral votes to get to the 270 votes to win that election. Returning again to Page 54, look at the elections from 1932 through 1944. F.D. Roosevelt won them all. In 1932 his opponent won 59 electoral votes. In 1936 his opponent won eight electoral votes. In the 1940 election his opponent won 82 total electoral votes. In the 1944 election his opponent, Thomas E. Dewey, won 99 electoral votes. All of these elections were over before the polls closed in the CST. This can be found in the column labeled, "Time Zones."

Looking back at the 1936 election, the total electoral vote count was 531. Roosevelt received 387 before the polls closed in the CST. Since Roosevelt only needed 266 to win, the election was over *before* the polls closed in the CST. The final electoral vote count gave Roosevelt 523 votes. His opponent, Alf Landon, only received eight. Page 56 shows a bar graph that gives a better view of how the candidates and the elections turned out. The political party that won the election and the differences in the electoral vote results are visualized as to how each candidate compared to each other. The legend explains the bars and numbers they represent. Note: the two even bars on the far-right show where the 270 electoral votes mark is. When the electoral vote count passes that mark the election is *over*. There is no mention of the popular vote because only electoral votes are reported.

The Western Vote Count When we talk about voting districts, states that have large populations will have more cities and will have more people living in clusters in and around those cities, and because of this, more voting districts are created. Because the western part of the country is where most of the farming and prairie states are, and also where those states that have a large share of the Rocky Mountain range located in them, the voting districts are few and far between. States like Montana, Wyoming, North and South Dakota, all have only three voting districts so they will each have three electoral votes. States like California, with 55 electoral votes, and Texas with 38, are swing states depending on the candidates. As I have already shown, because the election was already won their votes were not needed. It is a fact that politicians go where the most votes are, *electoral votes not popular votes.*

Battleground State Factors Some things that were not part of the Electoral College, but should be highlighted as to why the Electoral College can be manipulated: *battleground states.* As a rule, a "battleground state" has 10 or more electoral votes. If you review Page 46, look at the column labeled "States East of Mississippi River." The numbers represent the electoral vote count for each state. You will see that there are 15 states east of the Mississippi River that can be considered battleground states. West of the Mississippi River there are only six states that have similar numbers. There is nothing illegal about this, but for those campaigning in battleground states, there is a lot of money being spent. Television time and grandstand appearances are ways that state election officials can show a lot of favoritism to any candidate by controlling the cost for these venues. There are many states that have a large electoral vote count but they are not battleground states because traditionally they are supportive of one party over the other.

There is another reason that some states with large electoral vote counts are not battleground states. This is because, as I have shown already, their votes *are not needed.* California and Texas, with a total of 93 electoral votes, fall into this group. *But they are not battleground states. Why not*?? Texas and California, being western states, get very little attention as being battleground states because in 17 presidential elections their votes were *not needed.* Could it be that the political parties know this and will use their campaign money in only those states that are always winners?

The states in the EST and CST zones have 37 states, with a combined total of 410 electoral votes. The MST and PST zones have 13 states with a total electoral vote count of 128. Since a candidate needs only one more than half of 538, (270), in a winner-take-all election, the election can be over when the polls close in the CST.

I have made overtures as to how the Electoral College can be manipulated in presidential elections. Campaigning in battleground states, where the possibilities of fraud are present and the attention obtained from the media is the means to that end. Local officials have raised issues concerning the "Right to Vote" in recent elections that has caused major issues and challenges for some candidates. The 2020 election is the "firestorm of the times" because of the Electoral College. At the time of this writing, the cry of voter fraud has not let up in all of the state and national elections for over two years. Over the years, election rules have changed to benefit some candidates and cause problems for others. What is not clear is, are these changes coming from state election officials who are trying to affect voter turnout on Election Day, or are the national political parties raising issues that will benefit them the most?

The historical reports that will come out of the 2020 election may shed some light on that subject. My goal is not to uncover fraud but to uncover *and broadcast* why some voters that do vote and expect their votes to count for something should realize that their votes do nothing to affect the outcome of an election that is over because one of the candidates has reached *270 electoral votes* before all vote counting was done. Knowing this, how can we believe the advertisement at election time: "*Vote, Your Vote Counts!*"?

History "Knowing the events of the *past*, is knowing that changes made *today* will eliminate some pitfalls in the *future*." At this point we are not following the themes of democracy where the *vote of the public* picks our leaders. In the events of past elections, we see where using a winner-takes-all election system has reduced the voice and vote of over 128 million people down to 538 electoral votes that decides our presidential elections. It has, on 17 occasions, been reduced to where one vote over half of the total available electoral votes for the time *does* pick our national leaders. In putting this report together, the election results for the winners have been *only* the electoral vote, not the vote of the people. Even though we record the popular vote from each state, they are counted and collectively added together to get a total national *popular vote* count, but that resulting number *is not* used to select our leaders. The electoral vote is always the deciding vote.

It is true that when the counting is done for most elections, the candidate with the highest popular vote count has also received the most electoral votes. However, because we use the winner-take-all method in our state elections, and because the bottom line is the electoral vote being the prize, we are using one election to set up another election that will decide our president-elect. This election becomes a majority wins-type election because the candidate that wins one more electoral vote than his opponent wins the election. Elections held from 1789 to 1948, because of issues already discussed, were not only of a simpler method, but the only method because of conditions already shown. Logistics, communications and transportation were a few. After 1948, we have seen where all of those issues have changed and the *old* way is no longer the simplest.

However, out of almost 60 elections over the last 230 years, there were five elections going back to 1824, 1876, 1888, 2000, and 2016, where the popular vote was greater for the *losers* of those elections but the *winner* of those same elections received more electoral votes. I have highlighted the 2016 election because it is the most recent election and the outcome of that election shows how the western popular vote was *not* needed because by 8 pm in the CST the election was over. The fact that the winning candidate received over half of the electoral votes before the election was over changed the whole dynamics of the national election of 2016. The bottom line, by using the 538 electoral votes this way there will always be elections that will end like this.

538 electors cannot and should not speak for over 128 million voters. Why do we go through this same election process every four years? If it keeps several million voters from picking our leaders, then we will *always* have to accept the *will* of 538 electors.

Let's look at the Constitution again and this time I will try to interpret what is being said. Remember, this is how I am able to understand the writing of the Constitution.

Article II, Section 1, Paragraph 3. The Electors shall meet in their respective States, and vote by Ballot for two Persons... We now know that each state has a specific number of electors. We know that each elector receives one of the electoral votes from each state to take to Washington and personally vote for the candidate that won their election. Remember at the first election the candidate that received the most popular votes will become the president-elect and the candidate that is the runner-up will become the vice president.

...Of whom one at least shall not be an Inhabitant of the same State with themselves. The thought behind this is the elector cannot vote twice for the same candidate having voted in the popular voting.

And they shall make a List of all the Persons voted for, and of the Number of Votes for each... Could this "list" be the electoral votes from *all of the state elections that the winning candidate won?*

...which List they shall sign and certify, and transmit sealed to the Seat of the Government of the United States, directed to the President of the Senate. The President of the Senate shall, in the Presence of the Senate and House of Representative, open all the Certificates, and the Votes shall be counted and Ratified by Congress. With the signing of this list the electors are certifying the states' electoral vote count is accurate. Transmitting this sealed document to the seat of government is where today's electors, all 538 of them, make a trip to Washington DC and present the total vote count to the President of the Senate, who is always the current vice president of the United States. Where they will be opened in front of all of the congressmen there, to be ratified (made officially valid) as to the candidate that won the presidency. As a note: This will be the process that the *2020 election* will *always* be remembered for as the election that challenged our democracy and brought chaos to our Capital.

The Person having the greatest Number of Votes shall be the President, if such Number be a Majority of the whole Number of the Electors appointed This is where the number, 270 electoral votes, gets its power. "A Majority of the whole Number of the electors (538) appointed." One half plus one, 270 of 538, is the majority. In 1789 up through the 19th century, before the 1948 election, this trip was necessary because the electors and only a few people knew the outcome of the elections and this was how Congress officially became aware of the results of these elections. 230 years later, almost 60 presidential elections later, with the communications of today the people that make up Congress already know the results of any election on the day of the election. Then why is it necessary, when the election has been over for about two months, to do the same thing we *did at the first election*? Is this because of "Tradition?"

As I said, this subject is complex and confusing. Bringing everything together, we found out what an electoral vote is and how it is used in today's elections. We know that the total electoral vote count for the country is 538 and that once a candidate reaches 270 electoral votes that election is over and won. We know that in order for a candidate to win enough electoral votes he has to first win state elections with what is called the popular votes.

Today, with the communications systems we have, and the computers that can collect and count the state election results, and present the total vote for the country using television, results can be immediately presented on Election Day. The Electoral College is outdated, confusing, complex, and misunderstood by many and completely outdated as to the way things are done today. We have a voting process in place where the people can go to the voting polls, and with millions of other voters, using their one vote, elect *our* president. It is called, "The Popular Vote."

It is time to change before we have another "2020 election crash."

PART III
The Percentage Method

There is a simpler solution. We can keep the electoral vote and may not need an amendment to change the Constitution. If the electoral vote must be used, we should be using a method that does not reduce the popular vote to a token vote. If there is support for one candidate in the popular vote, that same support will be reflected in the electoral vote. Both voting systems will elect our presidents. This will require *all* the states to count *all* the votes that were cast for *all* the candidates. The winner-take-all element would not be part of this equation and the candidate that wins the popular vote will certainly win the electoral vote.

Percentage Method

As a note: Nebraska and Maine are two states using this method that divides the electoral votes between the candidates based on the percentage of the popular vote. This mathematical procedure is used when dividing something into a percentage of the total. Returning to the 2016 election and looking at the accumulated data for all the states in the EST elections on Page 47, find Florida. It is in the EST section for Trump and Clinton. I will use their data results to help explain the *"Percentage Method"* I am proposing. The calculations would be set up like the following:

First Find the total popular vote cast in Florida for both candidates. Trump's total is 4,617,886 + Clinton's total of 4,504,975 = 9,122,861, this is the total popular votes cast for both candidates for the State of Florida.

Second Find the percentage of the total vote each candidate won. This next calculation is as follows: Trump's percentage of the total is 4,617,886/9,122,861 = *51%*. Clinton's percentage of the total is 4,504,975/ 9,122,861= *49%*. See Pages 48 and 49.

Third Find how many electoral votes each state has. In this example, Florida has 29 electoral votes. Trump's percentage of this total is *29 x 51%* = *15* (rounded) electoral votes. Clinton's share is *29 x 49 %* = *14* (rounded) electoral votes. *15 +14* = *29*. Each candidate receives a percentage of the total electoral vote, not the total.

Instead of winner-take-all, each candidate would receive a percentage of the electoral vote that was equal to the percentage of the state's popular vote. Looking at Pages 48 – 53, the numbers in the far right column are the adjusted electoral vote count for each candidate, for each state, for each time zone they are in.

The columns marked *ADJ EVC*. The *Adjusted Electoral Vote Count* column is where the results are displayed. At the bottom of the ADJ EVC column find the total electoral vote counts that each candidate has won. Reviewing Pages 48 – 53, note that every state in all the time zones, in the columns labeled ADJ EVC, has all been adjusted the same as Florida's was. Mathematical rounding to a whole number was used. On Pages 57 and 58, there is an area in the middle of the page where the time zone totals are listed for both candidates. The numbers show the total EVC, the popular vote count, and the ADJ EVC total for each candidate. These results will best explain the "Percentage Method."

The electoral vote collected for each candidate shows their total vote count for the EVC and the ADJ EVC for each time zone. The total popular vote count for each candidate is also shown there. With this data one can see that Trump received 305 electoral votes, 62,982,066 popular votes and *265 adjusted electoral votes*. Clinton's total electoral vote count was 233, her total popular vote was 65,771,871 and her *adjusted electoral vote count was 273.*

Looking at the two adjusted counts for the two candidates for the 2016 election, it shows that Clinton's 273 adjusted vote count is greater than Trump's adjusted vote count of 265. This difference is because Clinton received 2,789,805 more popular votes than Trump. This was a close election therefore the difference of eight electoral votes would be expected. The most important lesson learned here is that the popular and the electoral vote count reflects the results of the voting of the *people.*

Because this is a *proposed system* this *did not happen.* I tried to show what *could* be. If we used a system like this there would be *no winner-take-all election. The election would not be over until all the votes were counted* across the country and that *would have* elected *our president.* These methods will keep our democracy *alive and kicking!!!*

CLOSING

In my opening statements I said that this subject matter was confusing and hard to understand. I tried to break it down and show *why* the things that became the model for the Electoral College in the beginning were due to *logistics, communications, and travel restrictions.* A second factor is that modern time zones didn't exist in 1789. Another issue that needed to be addressed was that the voting population of the time had very little experience in how an election should be held. The chosen electors did and became the solution to some of these problems. Electors became a large factor that was needed to organize and conduct an election to elect our presidents until the 1948 election.

It is my belief that the *winner-take-all* election and the *time zone factor* are the two reasons that in over 100 years of elections, the presidents, on their Election Days, were elected by only half of the country. There are several reasons that this occurs. One of the reasons is that the eastern part of the country has more people, therefore the electoral vote count for those states is higher. See Page 47. Another reason could be because the sun travels from east to west and the time zone effect comes into play. The eastern states start voting two and three hours sooner than the western states, therefore the results for the EST are reported three hours earlier. The main *reason* is if one candidate receives more than 270 electoral votes in the earlier time zones before the other candidate, then the election is over before all the voting is done across the country.

As I have shown, all the states have electoral votes, and with winner-take-all elections this is how the electoral votes are won by the candidates. Because the federal elections for our presidents use the electoral votes as the prize and the method used to elect our presidents is the same, these results will always be the norm.

In these many pages, I have explained the history of *why* the Electoral College was designed this way and *where* and *when* it took place. I talked about *who* the people were that handled and ran the early elections and *why* they were needed to do so. We have seen elections after 1948 where technology and logistics have changed, but the Electoral College election process rules have not. One can argue that we hold as many as 50 elections, plus Washington DC (not a state), plus the electoral vote before Congress, making a total of 52 elections before we get a president-elect. We already have the total national popular vote at the end of all the state elections. Why do we need to bring in the electoral votes?

The 2016 election and the 2020 election are harbingers of things to come. The 2016 election will always be remembered as the election where the losing candidate received 2,795,806 more popular votes than her opponent, but lost the election to him because he had won the most electoral votes. In reality, we do hold *two elections to get one president.*

History will show that the 2016 and 2020 elections came very close to destroying our democracy as we know it today. There was a similarity in both elections. The numbers tell the story. In the 2016 election, Trump's 305 electoral vote count to Clinton's 233 electoral vote count decided that election. In the 2020 election, Biden's 306 electoral votes to the incumbent President Trump's 232 electoral votes decided that election. Biden won 7,059,501 more popular votes than Trump. The difference between these two elections was that the 2020 election could not be called as being final when it was over because the final vote count in many states was being challenged by the losing candidate. I am *not* going to cover all the details of the 2020 election here, because history is still being written on this one. I will add one anecdote for the 2020 election that highlights my statement that the Electoral College election can be manipulated, and it will show how close we came to *overturning that election.*

I have made comments that the Electoral College can be manipulated. One event came out of the 2020 election that emphasizes this point. When Trump asked Georgia's secretary of state to, "get me 11,780 more votes." He was trying to change the outcome of the 2020 election! This number was the difference of the popular votes between Biden and Trump for that election. 2,473,633 - 2,461 854 = 11,779. Trump wanted Georgia's 16 electoral votes to upset the election. Someone should have told him that he would need more than Georgia's 16 electoral votes to win.

Can this system be manipulated? *Yes.* Can having more than two candidates in an election create havoc? *Yes.* Can having only 538 votes and only needing 270 votes to get elected president cause millions of voters to have their votes not count for anything? *Yes.* Then why do we need the Electoral College, why not just use the *popular vote count* to elect our president?

The *one good thing* that came out of the 2020 election was that this time the whole country's popular votes were counted and used *after* all the polls across the country closed. It is time to change, make the people's choice the final and *only* vote count that elects our president. Do away with the electoral vote and let democracy sing.

EXIT ACCOLADES

All the research credit is given to my smartphone and the historical databases it contains. The spelling assist was a large factor that led to the completion of this journal in 2023. I started it in 2019. I will never see the changes I feel *should happen*. Hopefully, if our educators get this or something like this into the hands of our young people, the Electoral College, like the Little Red School House, will fade into history. I thank Cajole D'Cunha associated with Monroe County Community College for his assistance and counseling on this project.

I hope this effort will help someone understand a little bit of the Constitution and the Electoral College.

Stan Rogers, 2023

Table of Contents

DATA RESOURCE INFORMATION

Ratification of the Constitution of all 50 States

STATE	DATE RATIFICATED	STATE	DATE RATIFICATED
Delaware	1787	Texas	1845
Pennsylvania	1787	Iowa	1846
New Jersey	1787	Wisconsin	1848
Georgia	1788	California	1850
Connecticut	1788	Minnesota	1858
Massachusetts	1788	Oregon	1859
Maryland	1788	Kansas	1861
South Carolina	1788	West Virginia	1863
New Hampshire	1788	Nevada	1864
Virginia	1788	Nebraska	1867
New York	1788	Colorado	1876
North Carolina	1789		
Rhode Island	1790	**TIME ZONE BEGINS**	1883
Vermont	1791	North Dakota	1889
Kentucky	1792	Montana	1889
Tennessee	1796	Washington	1889
Ohio	1803	Idaho	1890
Louisiana	1812	Wyoming	1890
Indiana	1816	Utah	1896
Mississippi	1817	Oklahoma	1907
Illinois	1818	New Mexico	1912
Alabama	1819	Arizona	1912
Maine	1820	Alaska	1959
Missouri	1821	Hawaii	1959
Arkansas	1836		
Michigan	1837		
Florida	1845		

States East of Mississippi River		States West of Mississippi River	
MAINE	4	MONTANA	3
DELAWARE	3	WYOMING	3
DC	3	NORTH DAKOTA	3
VERMONT	3	SOUTH DAKOTA	3
NEW HAMPSHIRE	4	ALASKA	3
RHODE ISLAND	4	IDAHO	4
WEST VIRGINIA	5	HAWAII	4
MISSISSIPPI	6	NEW MEXICO	5
CONNECTICUT	7	NEBRASKA	5
KENTUCKY	8	NEVADA	6
SOUTH CAROLINA	9	UTAH	6
ALABAMA	9	KANSAS	6
MARYLAND	10	IOWA	6
WISCONSIN	10	ARKANSAS	6
MASSACHUSETTS	11	OREGON	7
TENNESSEE	11	OKLAHOMA	7
INDIANA	11	LOUISIANA	8
VIRGINIA	13	COLORADO	9
NEW JERSEY	14	MINNESOTA	10
NORTH CAROLINA	15	MISSOURI	10
GEORGIA	16	ARIZONA	11
MICHIGAN	16	WASHINGTON	12
OHIO	18	TEXAS	38
PENNSYLVANIA	20	CALIFORNIA	55
ILLINOIS	20		
FLORIDA	29		
NEW YORK	29		
Total	308	Total	230

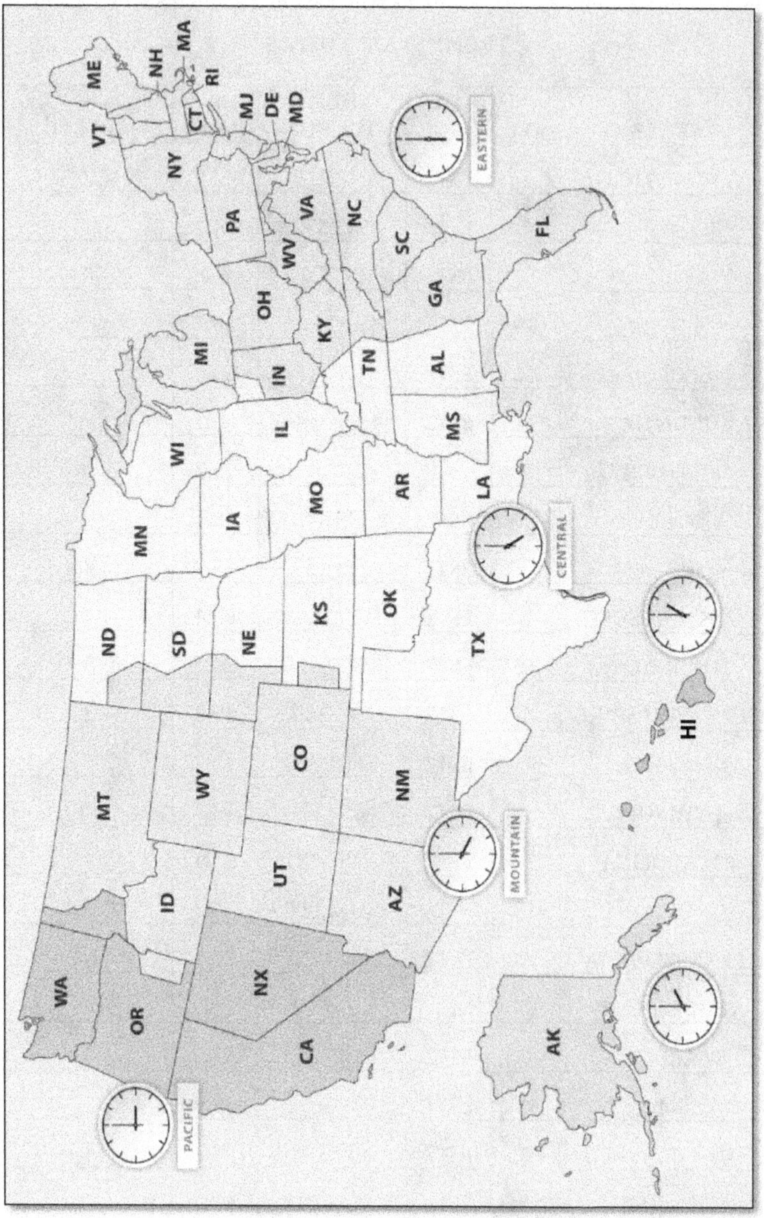
PACIFIC
MOUNTAIN
CENTRAL
EASTERN
WA
OR
CA
NX
ID
MT
WY
UT
AZ
CO
NM
ND
SD
NE
KS
OK
TX
MN
IA
MO
AR
LA
WI
IL
MS
MI
IN
TN
AL
OH
KY
GA
FL
SC
NC
VA
WV
PA
NY
VT
ME
NH
MA
RI
CT
MJ
DE
MD
AK
HI

STATE	EVC	TIME ZONE	TRUMP TOL POP	% WIN	ADJ EVC
TRUMP STATE TOTALS					
CONNECTICUT		ESTZ	673,215	42.9	3
DELAWARE		ESTZ	185,572	44.1	1
DC		ESTZ	12,723	4.3	0
FLORIDA	29	ESTZ	4,617,886	50.6	15
GEORGIA	16	ESTZ	2,089,104	52.6	8
INDIANA	11	ESTZ	1,557,286	60.1	7
KENTUCKY	8	ESTZ	1,202,971	65.7	5
MAINE		ESTZ	335,593	48.4	2
MARYLAND		ESTZ	943,169	35.9	4
MASSACHUSETTS		ESTZ	1,090,893	35.4	4
MICHIGAN	16	ESTZ	2,279,805	50.1	8
NEW HAMPSHIRE		ESTZ	345,789	49.8	2
NEW JERSEY		ESTZ	1,601,933	42.7	6
NEW YORK		ESTZ	2,819,534	38.2	11
N CAROLINA	15	ESTZ	2,362,631	51.9	8
OHIO	18	ESTZ	2,841,005	54.2	10
PENNSYLVANIA	20	ESTZ	2,970,733	50.4	10
RHODE ISLAND		ESTZ	180,543	41.6	2
S CAROLINA	9	ESTZ	1,155,389	57.5	5
VERMONT		ESTZ	95,367	34.9	1
W VIRGINIA	5	ESTZ	489,371	72.2	4
VIRGINA		ESTZ	1,769,443	47.2	6
TOTAL	**147**		**31,619,955**		**122 rounded**

2016 PRESIDENTIAL ELECTION

CLINTON STATE TOTALS

STATE	EVC	TIME ZONE	CLINTION TOL POP	% WIN	ADJ EVC
CONNECTICUT	7	ESTZ	897,572	57.1	4
DELAWARE	3	ESTZ	235,603	55.9	2
DC	3	ESTZ	282,830	95.7	3
FLORIDA		ESTZ	4,504,975	49.4	14
GEORGIA		ESTZ	1,877,963	47.3	8
INDIANA		ESTZ	1,033,126	39.8	4
KENTUCKY		ESTZ	626,834	34.3	3
MAINE	4	ESTZ	357,735	51.6	2
MARYLAND	10	ESTZ	1,677,928	64	6
MASSACHUSETTS	11	ESTZ	1,995,196	64.7	7
MICHIGAN		ESTZ	2,268,193	49.9	8
NEW HAMPSHIRE	4	ESTZ	348,521	50.2	2
NEW JERSEY	14	ESTZ	2,148,278	57.3	8
NEW YORK	29	ESTZ	4,556,124	61.8	18
N CAROLINA		ESTZ	2,189,316	48.1	7
OHIO		ESTZ	2,398,164	45.6	8
PENNSYLVANIA		ESTZ	2,926,441	49.6	10
RHODE ISLAND	4	ESTZ	252,525	58.3	2
S CAROLINA		ESTZ	855,373	42.5	4
VERMONT	3	ESTZ	178,179	65.1	2
W VIRGINIA		ESTZ	188,794	27.8	1
VIRGINIA	13	ESTZ	1,981,473	52.8	7
TOTAL	105		33,781,143		130 rounded

TRUMP STATES TOTALS					
STATE	EVC	TIME ZONE	TRUMP TOL POP	% WIN	ADJ EVC
ALABAMA	9	CSTZ	1,306,925	62.9	6
ARKANSAS	6	CSTZ	677,904	60.4	4
ILLINOIS		CSTZ	2,118,498	39.4	8
IOWA	6	CSTZ	798,923	51.8	3
KANSAS	6	CSTZ	656,009	57.2	3
LOUISIANA	8	CSTZ	1,178,004	58.1	5
MINNESOTA		CSTZ	1,322,891	45.4	5
MISSISSIPPI	6	CSTZ	678,457	58.3	4
MISSOURI	10	CSTZ	1,585,753	57.1	6
NEBRASKA	5	CSTZ	485,819	60.3	3
N DAKOTA	3	CSTZ	216,193	64.1	2
S DAKOTA	3	CSTZ	22,701	61.5	2
OKLAHOMA	7	CSTZ	947,934	65.3	6
TENNESSEE	11	CSTZ	1,522,925	61.1	7
TEXAS	38	CSTZ	4,681,590	52.6	20
WISCONSIN	10	CSTZ	1,405,467	47.9	5
TOTAL	128		19,810,993		88 rounded

275 ELECTORAL VOTES AT THIS TIME

2016 PRESIDENTIAL ELECTION

CLINTON STATES TOTALS

STATE	EVC	TIME ZONE	CLINTION TOL POP	% WIN	ADJ EVC
ALABAMA		CSTZ	718,084	34.6	3
ARKANSAS		CSTZ	378,729	33.8	2
ILLINOIS	20	CSTZ	2,977,498	55.4	12
IOWA		CSTZ	650,790	42.2	3
KANSAS		CSTZ	414,788	36.2	2
LOUISIANA		CSTZ	779,535	38.4	3
MINNESOTA	10	CSTZ	1,366,676	46.9	5
MISSISSIPPI		CSTZ	462,457	39.7	3
MISSOURI		CSTZ	1,054,889	38	4
NEBRASKA		CSTZ	273,858	34.3	2
N DAKOTA		CSTZ	95,526	27.8	1
S DAKOTA		CSTZ	117,442	34.0	1
OKLAHOMA		CSTZ	419,788	28.9	2
TENNESSEE		CSTZ	870,695	36.4	4
TEXAS		CSTZ	3,877,868	16.2	6
WISCONSIN		CSTZ	1,382,210	46.9	5
TOTAL	30		15,840,833		70 rounded

135 ELECTORAL VOTES AT THIS TIME

TRUMP STATES TOTALS

STATE	EVC	TIME ZONE	TRUMP POP TOL	% WIN	ADJ EVC
ARIZONA	11	MSTZ	1,252,401	51.9	6
COLORADO		MSTZ	1,202,484	47.3	4
IDAHO	4	MSTZ	409,055	68.3	3
MONTANA	3	MSTZ	279,240	61.1	2
NEW MEXICO		MSTZ	319,667	45.3	2
UTAH	6	MSTZ	515,231	62.4	4
WYOMING	3	MSTZ	489,371	72.2	2
TOTAL	27		4,467,449		23 rounded

302 ELECTORAL VOTES AT THIS TIME

STATE	EVC	TIME ZONE	TRUMP POP TOL	% WIN	ADJ EVC
ALASKA	3	PSTZ	163,387	58.4	2
CALIFORNIA		PSTZ	4,483,810	33.9	19
HAWAII		PSTZ	128,847	32.6	1
NEVADA		PSTZ	512,058	48.7	3
OREGON		PSTZ	784,403	43.9	3
WASHINGTON		PSTZ	1,221,747	41.2	5
TOTAL	3		7,294,252		33 rounded

305 ELECTORAL VOTES AT THIS TIME

CLINTON STATES TOTALS

STATE	EVC	TIME ZONE	CLINTON POP TOL	% WIN	ADJ EVC
ARIZONA		MSTZ	1,161,167	48.1	5
COLORADO	9	MSTZ	1,338,870	52.7	5
IDAHO		MSTZ	189,765	31.7	1
MONTANA		MSTZ	177,709	38.9	1
NEW MEXICO	5	MSTZ	385,234	54.7	3
UTAH		MSTZ	310,676	37.6	2
WYOMING		MSTZ	188,794	27.8	1
TOTAL	14		3,752,215		18 rounded

149 ELECTORAL VOTES AT THIS TIME

STATE	EVC	TIME ZONE	CLINTON POP TOL	% WIN	ADJ EVC
ALASKA		PSTZ	116,454	41.6	1
CALIFORNIA	55	PSTZ	8,753,788	66.1	36
HAWAII	4	PSTZ	266,891	67.4	3
NEVADA	6	PSTZ	539,260	51.3	3
OREGON	7	PSTZ	1,002,106	56.1	4
WASHINGTON	12	PSTZ	1,742,718	58.8	7
TOTAL	84		12,421,217		54 rounded

233 ELECTORAL VOTES AT THIS TIME

Year	Name of President Elect	Winner Popular Vote / MM	Winner EV	Loser EV	EV Difference	Electoral Votes Need to Win	Time Zone Election Won In
1916	Wilson	9 MM	277	254	23	266	PTZ
1920	Harding	16 MM	404	127	268	266	CTZ
1924	Coolidge	16MM	382	136	246	266	CTZ
1928	Hoover	21MM	444	87	375	266	ETZ
1932	F.D. Roosevelt	23MM	472	59	413	266	ETZ
1936	F.D. Roosevelt	28MM	532	8	524	266	ETZ
1940	F.D. Roosevelt	27MM	449	82	367	266	ETZ
1944	F.D. Roosevelt	26MM	432	99	333	266	ETZ
1948	Truman	24MM	303	189	114	266	PST
1952	Eisenhower	34MM	442	89	353	266	CST
1956	Eisenhower	36MM	457	73	384	266	EST
1960	Kennedy	34MM	303	219	84	269	PST
1964	Johnson	43MM	486	52	434	270	EST
1968	Nixon	32MM	301	191	110	270	CST
1972	Nixon	47MM	520	17	503	270	EST
1976	Carter	41MM	297	240	57	270	CST
1980	Reagan	44MM	489	49	440	270	EST
1984	Reagan	54MM	525	13	512	270	EST
1988	G.H. Bush	49MM	426	111	315	270	EST
1992	Clinton	45MM	370	168	202	270	CST
1996	Clinton	47MM	379	159	220	270	CST
2000	G.W. Bush	50MM	271	266	5	270	PST
2016	Trump	63MM	305	277	77	270	CST
2020	Biden	81MM	306	232	74	270	PST

DESCRIPTION OF COLUMN TERMS

Year	Name of President Elect
Name of President Elect	The Name of the Winning Candidate.
Winner's Popular Vote	The Popular Vote count Rounded to Largest Million Count.
Winner EV	The Electoral Vote Count the Winning Candidate Received.
Loser EV	The Electoral Votes Count the Loser received.
Difference EV	The Difference of Electoral Votes between the Winning and Losing Candidate.
Electoral Votes Needed to Win	One half of the country's Electoral votes total at the time. The 266 total to win is one half of 531 plus one. The 270 total to win is one half of 538 plus one. The increase was when Alaska and Hawaii joined the Union and ratified the Constitution in 1959. Washington DC was awarded 3 Electoral votes in 1961.
Time Zone Election Won	When a candidate reached the 266 or 270 Electoral Vote Count the losing Candidate cannot receive enough Votes to win the Presidency therefore the election is over.
Note 1	As of the 2020 Election the Democrats won 14 elections while the Republicans have won 13.
Note 2	As of the 2020 Election there has been 21 elections won when the polls closed in the CTZ.
Note 3	As of the 2020 Election there have been ONLY 6 Elections that have NOT BEEN DECIDED until all the poles have closed crossed the country. Most of those were due to recounts.

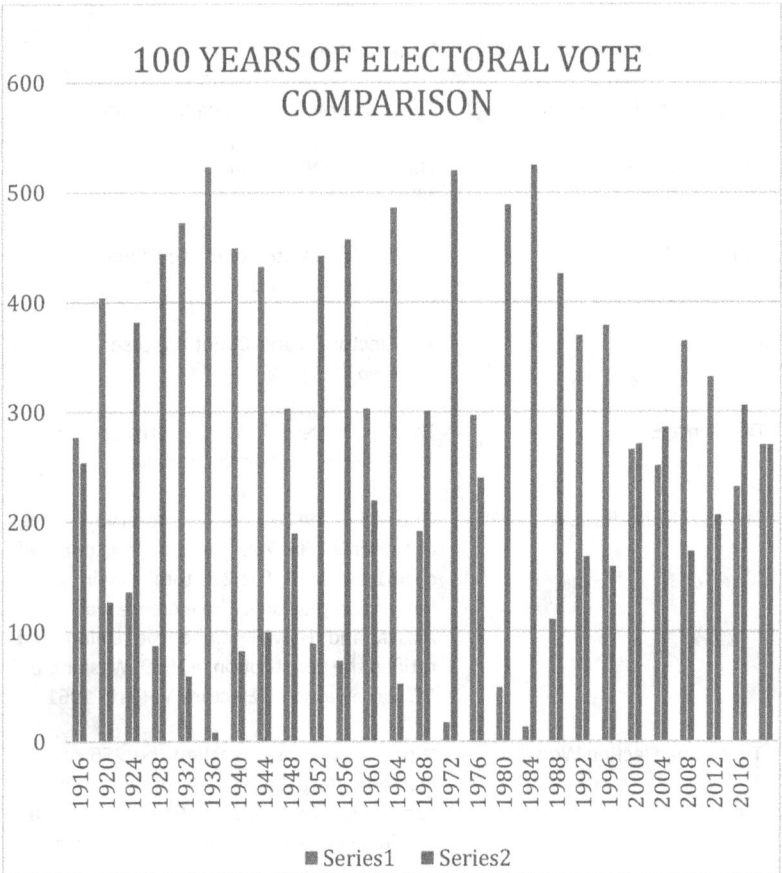

100 YEARS OF ELECTORAL VOTE COMPARISON

BAR GRAFT LEDGER

- BARS ON THE LEFT REPRESENT THE DEMOCRAT CANDIDATE
- BARS ON THE RIGHT REPRESENT THE REPUBLICATION CANDIDATE
- THE DATES ACROSS THE BOTTOM ARE ELECTION YEARS
- THE COLUMN OF NUMBERS ON THE LEFT 0 THRU 600 IS THE ELECTORAL NUMBERED
- THE TWO COLUMNS ON THE GRAPH ON THE FAR RIGHT REPRESENT 270 ELECTORAL VOTE THAT SIGNAL THE ELECTION IS OVER.

2016 Presidential Election

Trump State Totals

Trump's totals for all the Time Zones

Time Zone	ESTZ	CSTZ	MSTZ	PSTZ
Electoral Vote Total /TZ	147	128	27	3
Popular Vote/TZ	31,619,955	19,810,933	4,467,449	7,294,252
Adjusted EVC/TZ	122	88	23	33
Total Electoral Vote Count		305		
Total Popular Vote Count		63,192,589		
Total Adjusted Electoral Vote Count		265		

DEFINITION

TIME ZONES	Eastern	Central	Mountain	Pacific
EVC		The Electoral Vote Count		
TOTAL POPULAR VOTE		Trump's Total Popular Vote Count for the Country		
ADJ EVC		The % of the State Electoral Vote Count Trump would have won using the PERCENTAGE METHOD outlined in the Text.		

2016 Presidential Election

Clinton's State Totals

Clinton's totals for all the Time Zones

Time Zone	ESTZ	CSTZ	MSTZ	PSTZ
Electoral Vote Total /TZ	105	30	14	84
Popular Vote/TZ	33,781,143	15,480,833	3,752,215	12,421,317
Adjusted EVC/TZ	130	70	18	54
Total Electoral Vote Count		233		
Total Popular Vote Count		65,255,408		
Total Adjusted Electoral Vote Count		273		

DEFINITION

TIME ZONES	Eastern	Central	Mountain	Pacific
EVC		The Electoral Vote Count		
TOTAL POPULAR VOTE		Clinton's Total Popular Vote Count for the Country		
ADJ EVC		The % of the State Electoral Vote Count Clinton would have won using the PERCENTAGE METHOD outlined in the Text.		

Final Words from The Author

When I read or have read a book, I look for the compassion in the words from the author. In most cases this will come from the subject matter and jump right out at you. Obviously, in this case the subject matter is very cut and dry. In my youth, decades ago, I had no interest. As a young father my interest was in my career in my family. As I matured into my older years, my thoughts and interest changed to what they are today. People.

Why I chose the subject of political Presidential Election is still a mystery, except I saw how a gift from the Constitution eliminated millions of people and reduced the value of this gift to nothing. I could not let this go until I said something. I surprised myself with the results of the data. The one thing I found is that this action does not support only one party. I did not elaborate on this, but I did show that the 2016 election and the 2020 election were mirror images of each other and both political parties benefited. The supporting data shows that this action has happened over the years.

Democracy is the compassion of this article. Google's definition of Democracy is, and I quote, "A system of government by the WHOLE population or all the eligible members of a state, or in this rendering the UNITED STATES." IF DEMOCRACY is going to last for another 100 years, then a CHANGE to the ELECTORAL COLLEGE must happen.

www.ingramcontent.com/pod-product-compliance
Lightning Source LLC
Chambersburg PA
CBHW060520280326
41933CB00014B/3038